Explore Your Senses

HEARING

by Laurence Pringle

BENCHMARK **B**OOKS

MARSHALL CAVENDISH
NEW YORK

The author wishes to thank Dr. Edward J. Kormondy, Chancellor and Professor of Biology (retired), University of Hawaii-Hilo/West Oahu for his careful reading of this text and his thoughtful and useful comments. The text has been improved by Dr. Kormondy's notes, however the author assumes full responsibility for the substance of the work, including any errors that may appear.

Benchmark Books
Marshall Cavendish Corporation
99 White Plains Road
Tarrytown, NY 10591

Library of Congress Cataloging-in-Publication Data
Pringle, Laurence P.
Hearing / by Laurence Pringle.
p. cm. — (Explore your senses)
Included bibliographical references and index.
Summary: Describes the parts of the ear and how they function and discusses the
ways animals hear, maintaining balance, taking care of your hearing, and more.
ISBN 0-7614-0735-9
1. Hearing—Juvenile literature. [1. Hearing. 2. Ear. 3. Senses and sensation.]
I. Title. II. Series: Pringle, Laurence P.   Explore your senses.
QP462.2.P75   1999   612.8'5—dc21   98-28041   CIP   AC

Printed in Hong Kong

6   5   4   3   2   1

Photo research by Linda Sykes Picture Research, Hilton Head, SC

Cover photo: The Stock Market / Richard Gross
Picture credits: The photographs in this book are used by permission and through the courtesy of: Corbis-Bettmann: 29. Culver Pictures: 6 (top), 6 (bottom). Photo Edit: 5 (bottom left) Michael Newman; 11 (right) Bonnie Kamin; 22 Nova Stock; 28 Robin Sachs. Photo Researchers: 4 (middle) Simon Pollard; 16 CNRI/Science Photo Library; 19 Prof. A. Motta/Univ. La Spienza, Rome. The Image Bank: 4 (top right) Liysa King; 4 (bottom) Luis Veiga; 5 (top right) Terje Rakke; 5 (bottom right); 7 Pete Turner; 12 Steve Satushek; 24 Joseph Van Os; 26 Turner and Devries. Stock Boston: 11 (left) Frank Siteman; 14 John Cancalos; 27 Alexander Tsiaras.

Contents

Your Sense of Hearing   4

Sounds Travel in Waves   6

When You Speak   8

Waves of Sound   10

How Loud Is It?   12

The Outer Ear   14

Your Amazing Ear Bones   16

The Inner Ear   18

Hearing With Your Brain   20

Keeping Your Balance   22

Animal Ears   24

Extending Our Hearing   26

Taking Care of Your Hearing   28

Glossary   30

Index   32

Close your eyes, and listen. Make a mental list of all the sounds you hear. You might hear loud sounds: a shout or the blare of a car horn. You might hear quiet sounds: a whisper, the purr of a cat, leaves rustling in a breeze.

Our sense of hearing is vital in many ways. Our hearing helps keep us safe, for example, when we hear the sound of an approaching car that we cannot see. It helps us locate a kitten that was accidentally shut in a closet. Perhaps most important, it helps us communicate with one another through speech.

Our sense of hearing also enriches our lives with the soothing sounds of nature—waves lapping a sandy shore, crickets chirping, birds singing. The sound of music can make us feel sad, or lift our spirits high.

People can hear a wide range of sounds, from the annoying whine of a mosquito to the loud skirl of a bagpipe. However, there are some animals—including bats and elephants—that make and hear sounds that we cannot hear.

Usually it is said that humans have five senses: sight, hearing, taste, smell, and touch. However, the sense of balance is sometimes called a sixth sense. It allows us to move safely without tipping over, and to keep right side up. Part of our hearing system helps us keep our balance. This makes our sense of hearing doubly important.

Your Sense of Hearing

Sounds can soothe, excite, warn, or annoy us.
Clockwise from upper left: ocean waves, howling dog,
jackhammer, harmonica, young bird in nest, and
cricket. A male cricket makes chirping sounds by
rubbing one wing cover against the other.

Toss a pebble into the still water of a puddle. The water splashes, and circles of ripples spread outward. The little waves get smaller and smaller as they spread outward.

Smack the palms of your hands together— hard—and something similar happens. Just as a pebble causes water to move, your hands cause air to move. Just as ripples spread outward in water, waves of disturbed air spread outward. The farther they spread, the smaller these sound waves become. The sound of smacking your hands together is loud to you, but is a very faint sound to someone listening across a field.

Sound waves travel through air, metal, and water. If you swim underwater, you can hear sounds, including the calls of fish. Some groups of fish are named for the sounds they make—drums, grunts, and croakers!

Long ago, people believed that sound traveled through the air but they could not prove it. In the mid-1600s, an Irish chemist named Robert Boyle found a way. He put a ticking watch inside an air-tight jar. Then he slowly pumped air out of the jar. The sound of the watch grew faint. When all of the air was removed, the watch was still running but made no sound at all.

Waves of sound travel fastest through metal. They travel nearly five times faster in water than in air. In

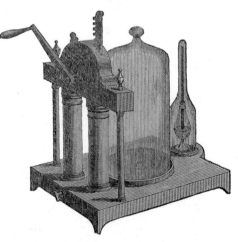

With a device like this, Robert Boyle proved that sound waves travel through air.

Sound Travels in Waves

the air, waves of sound still travel fast, about 760 miles (1,216 kilometers) an hour. That's at least ten times faster than you have traveled in a car. It is also 1,100 feet (3,300 meters) per second. However, sound moves slowly compared with the speed of light. Light travels 186,282 miles (298,051 kilometers) *a second*. That's nearly a million times faster than sound.

You may have noticed this difference between the speed of sound and the speed of light. At a fireworks display, you see the flash of light of an explosion high in the sky before you hear the sound. In the daytime you may hear the sound of a high-flying airplane. You look where the sound is coming from but see no aircraft. Then you see it in another part of the sky. Light travels so fast, you see the airplane where it *is*, but the slower-moving sound that reaches your ears is from the place the airplane *was*.

The electrical energy of lightning heats air and causes thunder. To find out how close lightning is to you, count the seconds after it flashes until you hear the sound of thunder. Divide the number of seconds by five to find the distance in miles.

As you speak or just hum, press your fingers against the front of your throat. You will feel vibrations there. When you want to speak, your vocal cords vibrate. The vibrations disturb the air. Waves of disturbed air—sound waves—then come out of your mouth.

Think of all the sounds you can make—whispers and shouts, high squeaky sounds and deep gruff sounds, plus all of the words you speak in everyday conversation. This rich variety of sounds is possible because of teamwork by several parts of your body.

Suppose you want to tell a story to a friend. As your brain chooses words, it sends a stream of nerve impulses to muscles in your chest, throat, jaws, and mouth. Muscles in your upper chest push air from your lungs up your windpipe, which is also called the trachea. At the top of the windpipe is your voicebox, or *larynx*. Muscles in the larynx move rapidly and change the steady flow of air into a series of puffs of air that pass over your vocal cords.

Air rushing over your vocal cords makes them vibrate and produce sound waves. Muscles attached to these cords control their length and how tightly they are stretched. When the vocal cords are pulled tight, the vibrations produce a high-pitched sound. When the cords are loosened they make a low sound. The vocal cord muscles make split-second changes that alter the vibrations of the cords—and

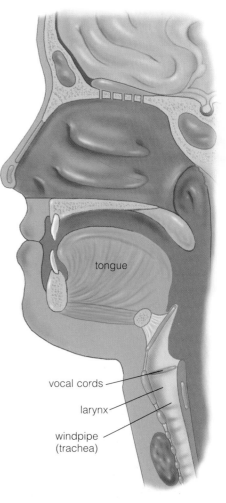

tongue

vocal cords

larynx

windpipe
(trachea)

When You Speak

the sounds that rise out of your throat.

Before sounds leave your mouth, however, they are affected by the hollow space in your mouth, and also by your tongue, teeth, and lips. Notice that your tongue moves as you talk. It affects the size and shape of the hollow space of your mouth—and this affects the sounds you make.

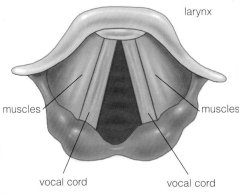

Watch as a friend talks and notice how the shape of his or her mouth changes. Muscles that change the shape of the mouth also affect the sound waves that emerge. You may have discovered this already. Perhaps a dentist injected a medical drug into your jaw muscles when filling a tooth cavity. Some of the muscles of your jaw and mouth became numb, and you found that you could not speak very clearly.

The vocal cords of children are all about the same size, so the voices of boys and girls sound much alike. This changes, however, when they grow to be adults. The vocal cords of males nearly double in size. They are about an inch long. The cords of women are shorter, about a half-inch long. Because of this difference it is usually easy to tell the voice of a man from a woman.

The vocal cords of teenage boys often grow rapidly. They have to learn again how to control the sounds they make. Sometimes their voices squeak. We say their voices are changing, and they are, to a much deeper sound.

Sound waves are invisible. If you drew a picture of one, it would look like a wavy line. Just as waves in water have highs and lows, so with sound waves. The distance from a wave's high point to its low point is called the wave's *amplitude*. The greater the amplitude, the louder the sound. As a sound wave travels, its amplitude decreases and the sound becomes more and more faint.

Another measurement of sound waves is their *wavelength*. It is the distance from the peak of one wave to the next peak (or from one trough to the next). The longer the wavelength, the fewer vibrations there are in each second. The number of sound vibrations in a second can also be expressed as the sound wave's *frequency*.

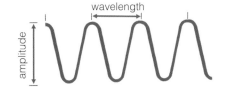

A sound wave with long wavelengths always has a low frequency. Sounds from such waves include the rumble of distant thunder, the low hoot of a great horned owl, and the oopah-oopah of a tuba.

A sound wave with short wavelengths always has a high frequency. This kind of sound wave produces such sounds as a shrill whistle, the shrieks of two cats in a fight, and the high notes of a flute.

A sound's frequency—the number of vibrations in a second—is expressed in units called *hertz*. (Hertz are named for Heinrich Hertz, a German scientist who was the first to broadcast and receive radio waves.) Humans can hear a wide range of sound

Waves of Sound

frequencies. A child can hear from 20 to 20,000 hertz. As people grow older they hear less and less of high-frequency sounds. Elderly people usually cannot hear sounds above 12,000 hertz. Older bird-watchers say that they can no longer hear the songs of certain birds, and so have to rely on sight alone to identify them.

Many animals hear sounds that are either above or below the human hearing range. You may have heard of a "silent" dog whistle. Dogs can detect sounds with frequencies as high as 30,000 hertz—well above human hearing. Dogs hear a shrill, high-pitched sound, but to people the whistle is silent.

A tuba produces low-frequency sound waves, while a flute produces high-frequency sound waves.

Scientists use a unit called the bel to measure a sound's loudness. The bel is named after Alexander Graham Bell, who invented the telephone. An increase of one bel means a sound has become ten times louder. Since the bel is a big unit, the loudness of different sounds is usually expressed in tenths of a bel, or *decibels*.

Devices that measure decibels actually record the pressure that sound waves make on a sensitive surface. A soft whisper pushes only a little against a surface. It measures about 20 decibels. When people talk, their sound waves exert a pressure of between 45 and 60 decibels.

Very loud sounds measure more than a hundred decibels. You may not even need a special device to detect them. Sometimes you can actually feel the sound waves hitting your body. Young people at rock music concerts experience this when they stand close to the sound system's speakers.

The decibel level at a rock concert may reach 130 decibels—loud enough to cause pain in the ears. Any sound above 90 decibels is dangerously loud. Listening to loud sounds for many hours can cause permanent harm to a person's hearing. Rock musicians, factory workers, and others who are often exposed to loud sounds usually lose part of their sense of hearing.

Very loud sounds are often called noise pollution.

Whether a sound is from a whisper or loud music, the pressure of its sound waves can be measured in decibels.

How Loud Is It?

One example is the roar of jet airplanes landing and taking off.
People who fight against noise pollution need to know how loud
a sound is, so they use devices that measure decibels.

Sound Strength in Decibels	
rustling leaves, flowing stream	15
whisper	20-30
conversation	45-60
normal level of sounds in an office	50
vacuum cleaner	75
electric shaver	85
screaming child	90
jackhammer or subway train	100
gas-powered lawn mower	105
snowmobile from driver's seat	110
rock band	120
level at which sound causes pain	130
80 feet (24 meters) from jet airplane taking off	140
rocket being launched 150 feet (45 meters) away	180

Here's a riddle that many people have puzzled over and debated: "If a tree falls in a forest and no one is there to hear it crash, would there be any sound?"

At first thought, many people find this a silly question and say, "Of course there is a sound!" But the question deserves a second thought. Its answer depends on understanding both sound waves and hearing. The pages before this one have explained how sound waves are made, how they travel, and how they are measured. Now it is time to explore how sound waves are actually heard.

We call the fleshy objects on the sides of our heads ears. Scientists sometimes call them *auricles*, or *pinnae*. They are made of skin and a flexible material called *cartilage*. Your ears are the most visible and largest parts of your hearing system—but they are the least important part. If you did not have your auricles you could still hear well.

Nevertheless, your ear's curving ridges and valleys do help you hear. Sound waves are reflected off them, then sent into the ear canal. The sound waves are changed so that you can tell whether sounds are coming from front or behind, or from above or below. Sometimes we help our ears intercept sound waves by turning our head toward the sound, or by cupping a hand behind an ear. Unlike many mammals, we cannot move our ears.

Jack rabbits have highly flexible ears that can turn toward the source of a sound.

The Outer Ear

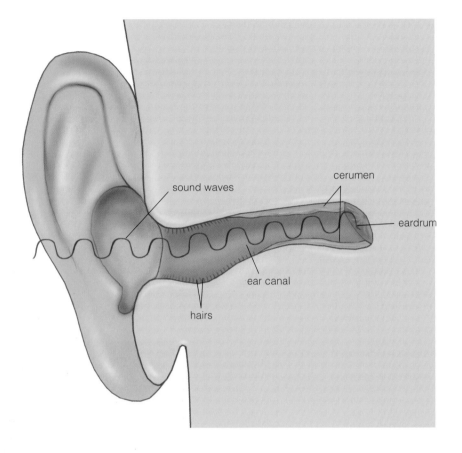

sound waves

cerumen

eardrum

ear canal

hairs

Sound waves first enter the outer ear canal, which is about an inch long. They bounce off the walls, vibrate more quickly, and grow louder than when they entered the canal.

Each of your two ear canals is lined with tiny hairs that trap bits of dirt. Your ears are also protected from dust and germs by wax that is secreted by tiny glands in the skin of the canals. The sticky earwax is called *cerumen*.

Your ear canals end in a wall, but it is no ordinary wall. It is a thin membrane stretched tightly across the ear canal. It is the *eardrum*, a vital part of your sense of hearing.

Humans have 206 bones in their bodies. Some are more important than others. Among the most vital are six tiny bones, three in each ear. Joined together, all three bones measure about a quarter of an inch in length. They are the smallest bones in our body. However, without these little bones you could not hear.

In each ear, the bone called the *hammer* is attached to the inner surface of the eardrum. The hammer is connected to the *anvil* bone, and the anvil is joined to the *stirrup* bone. Each bone is named for its shape. The stirrup bone, in particular, at its end looks like the place a tiny horseback rider would put a foot. This part of the stirrup bone is attached to a membrane that is stretched across the *oval window*, the opening to the inner ear.

When sound waves cause the eardrum to vibrate, the vibrations make the little bones move. The bones actually increase, or *amplify*, the vibrations of the eardrum. This makes it possible for you to hear whispers and other quiet sounds.

However, a person's hearing can be harmed if a very loud sound is amplified by his or her ear bones. Muscles in the middle ear defend against this. Some tighten the eardrum to reduce its vibrations. Others move the stirrup bone away from the oval window. If these muscles have time to react to a loud sound, they help protect delicate ear parts from harm.

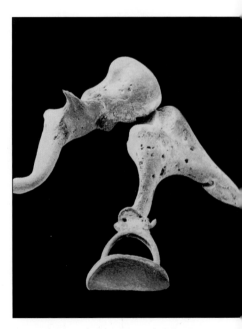

The three tiny bones in each ear are the hammer (top), anvil (middle), and stirrup (bottom).

Your Amazing Ear Bones

The middle ear also has a defense against changes in air pressure. If the middle ear had no connection to air outside, the eardrum or ear bones might be harmed when the air pressure changed outside. A narrow tube prevents this from happening. The *eustachian tube*, about two inches long, runs from the middle ear to an opening in the back of the throat.

The end of the eustachian tube in your throat usually opens when you yawn or swallow. This tube plays an important role when you fly on a jet airliner. Air pressure changes in the airplane when it rises to high altitudes and changes again when the plane lands. You may feel pain if the air pressure within your middle ears differs from the outside air pressure. Also, you cannot hear well because your eardrums cannot vibrate freely without equal air pressure on both sides.

By swallowing, yawning, or blowing your nose, you help air rise up the eustachian tube to the middle ear. The air pressure within changes to match the pressure outside. You feel better and hear better.

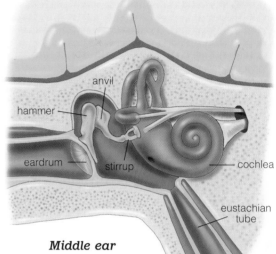

Middle ear

When the tiny stirrup bone quivers with sound vibrations, it passes them on to the oval window and into a remarkable organ called the *cochlea*. About the size of your fingertip, the cochlea looks like a spiral snail shell. (Its name, cochlea, comes from the Latin word for snail.)

The coiled tubes of the cochlea are filled with a fluid called *lymph*. Fluids do not vibrate as easily as air, but the ear bones amplify the sound vibrations they receive and deliver powerful vibrations to the little *oval window* of the cochlea. The vibrations travel through the lymph.

The vibrations reach a long membrane covered

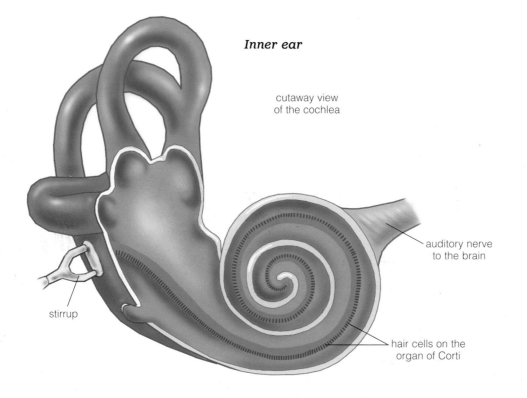

Inner ear

cutaway view
of the cochlea

auditory nerve
to the brain

stirrup

hair cells on the
organ of Corti

with about 16,000 hairlike nerve cells. It is called the *organ of Corti*, after the Italian biologist Alfonso Corti, who first studied this part of the cochlea with a microscope and described it. The hair cells are arranged in four parallel rows. Vibrations passing through the lymph cause the membrane to move, and this movement causes the hair cells to bend.

Each of these fine hairs is tuned to a particular sound vibration. Whenever a hair is moved, an electrical impulse or message is sent to the *auditory nerve*. Messages about sound vibrations are carried to the brain. That is where hearing actually happens.

Microscopic hair cells, shown in yellow, are arranged in rows on the organ of Corti. The hair cells detect sound vibrations, then send messages about the sounds to the brain.

The sound waves that enter your ears go through remarkable changes before becoming sounds you hear. First they are changed to physical vibrations by your eardrums, then to fluid vibrations in the cochlea and, finally, to electrical nerve impulses.

The nerve impulses travel instantly to the *medulla*, at the back of your brain. The medulla acts as a sort of switchboard, sending messages to other parts of the brain. Your ears take in every sound in their hearing range, then your brain makes split-second choices about which sounds can be ignored and which need attention.

Some choices may affect your safet, or other matters that are important to you. As you cross a street, a car's horn suddenly blares, and you recognize it as a warning. Or, out of all the sounds at a noisy shopping mall, you hear your name called by a friend's familiar voice.

These instant choices about sounds are possible because your brain has areas where sound memories are stored. Two of these areas are called the *temporal lobes*. They are located just behind your ears.

You have been storing sound memories since before you were born. As a fetus in your mother's womb, you heard the sound of her heartbeat. You probably heard the faint sounds of voices and music, too. By the time you are an adult, you can

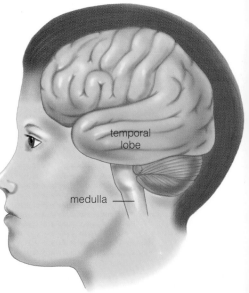

temporal lobe

medulla

Hearing With Your Brain

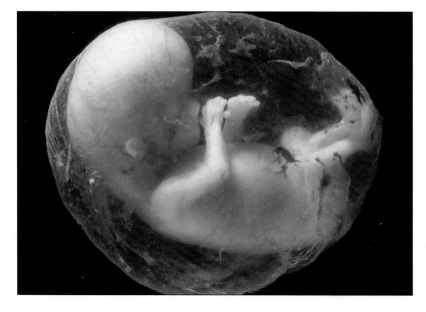

Humans begin to hear before they are born, after developing for several months in the womb.

recognize about a half million different sounds.

Each side of your brain receives some nerve messages from both ears. Receiving sounds from two ears is important. When a sound comes from one side, it reaches the ear on that side first. Your brain is able to detect tiny differences in the time of arrival of sounds at each ear. This helps you tell the direction a sound comes from, and judge how far away the sound was made.

You can also hear one sound with one ear, another sound with the other ear, and pay some attention to both. This isn't true, however, when you hear two people talking. Understanding speech is very important to humans, and their brains can only concentrate on one spoken message at a time.

When you dance, play sports, or just leap quickly to your feet, you usually keep your balance. Your brain sends messages to your muscles, which make quick adjustments to keep you upright. We take this sense of balance for granted. But humans would not be able to balance themselves on two legs or walk if they did not have special organs in their inner ears.

Next to the cochlea are three loops of tubing called the *semicircular canals*. Like the cochlea, these tubes are filled with lymph. They also contain hairlike nerve cells. When you move your head, the fluid moves and then the hairs move, sending nerve messages to the brain.

The three semicircular canals are set at different angles. Each one detects different motions of your head: up and down, side to side, or forward and backward. Together the three loops keep the brain informed about the position and movement of your head.

At the base of the semicircular canals are two other structures that help your balance. They are the *utricle* and the *saccule*. They contain lymph, hair cells, and also tiny crystals that are embedded in a jellylike membrane. The crystals are called *otoliths*. When you move your head, the otoliths cause the hair cells to move. Messages about your head's movement are sent to your brain.

Graceful ice skating would not be possible without the balancing organs of the inner ears (location shown in red below.)

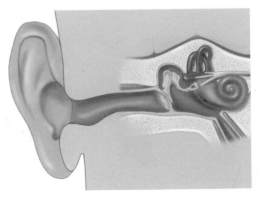

Keeping Your Balance

Otoliths are small but heavy. They are affected by *gravity*, the force that pulls everything toward the center of the Earth. When you turn yourself upside down—for example, while swimming underwater—their movements help you tell up from down. Otoliths cannot help in space, however, because usually there is no gravity.

While playing you have probably whirled around and around, then felt dizzy and unsteady on your feet. This happens because the whirling also affects the lymph in your semicircular canals. The lymph continues to move for a while after you have stopped. Messages from the hair cells tell your brain that you are still moving, while messages from your eyes say you have stopped. The result of these confusing messages is a brief dizzy feeling.

By keeping track of the horizon, your sense of sight also helps you tell up from down. However, without the balancing organs in your inner ears, you could not walk far or even get to your feet and stand easily.

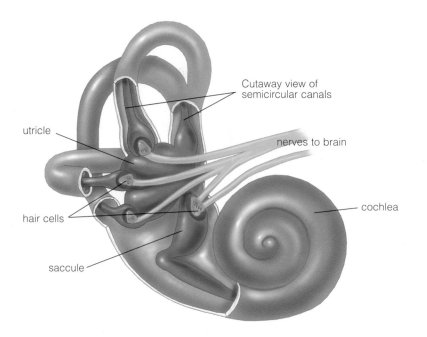

Cutaway view of semicircular canals

utricle

nerves to brain

hair cells

cochlea

saccule

$\mathbf{R}$emember the question asked earlier: "If a tree falls in a forest and no one is there to hear it crash, would there be a sound?" Now you know that sound waves are just disturbed air in motion. They become sounds when they are received by a human eardrum and become nerve messages sent to a person's brain.

However, a forest with no people in it may still have hundreds or even thousands of listeners. Plants cannot hear but many animals can. Mammals, birds, and a variety of other creatures, including insects, have ways of making and receiving sound waves. For a falling tree to make no sound, a large area of forest would have to be without animal life.

Animals make sounds in order to communicate with others of their kind. The songs of male birds, for example, attract females and also defend a home territory against other males. Both male and female birds give alarm calls that warn of danger. And owls also rely on a keen sense of hearing to catch food.

Some owls have tufts of feathers that look like ears but are not. The openings to their ear canals are just small holes on the sides of their heads, well hidden beneath feathers. Owls, which hunt in darkness, have exceptionally good hearing.

Insect-eating bats also rely on their sense of hearing for catching food. A frightened bat, trying

Owl ears, hidden beneath feathers, do not match exactly. One is slightly higher than the other. This difference affects the sounds received by the owl's inner ears, and helps the owl locate prey in the dark.

to scare you away, emits high-pitched squeaks that you can hear. It makes other squeaks you cannot hear. Most bat sounds are far beyond our hearing range. Such sounds are called *ultrasounds* (ultra means high). People hear in the range of 20 to 20,000 hertz. Bats hear in a range of 20,000 to 100,000 hertz.

Flying at night, a bat emits ten or more bursts of ultrasound each second. The sound waves bound off objects. Some are reflected back to the bat. A bat's face and especially its ears are shaped to take in these echoes.

From the echoes a bat gets some kind of picture in its brain of what lies ahead. It avoids flying into trees and other large things; it also avoids twigs, wires, and other small obstacles. When you see a bat flying toward a moth or other flying insect, the bat may be squeaking 200 times a second as it closes in for the kill. To your ears, the bat is silent.

Experts on hearing say that it is a good thing that people cannot hear very-low-frequency sounds. If we could, we would hear a steady jumble of sounds from the workings of our own bodies!

Many of the sounds of our muscles working, blood flowing, and so on are below our hearing range. They are called *infrasounds* (infra means below). Elephants, crocodiles, and alligators communicate with infrasounds. People can hear elephants give low, rumbling calls, but lower elephant calls that travel as far as 6 miles (9.6 kilometers) go undetected by humans.

Humans can hear a wide range of sounds but their ears are most sensitive to a frequency around 1,000 hertz. This is the frequency of people talking. Being able to hear speech of other people is very important.

There are also times when it is important to detect sounds we do not usually hear. So people have tried to extend their hearing. About three centuries ago, a Frenchman invented the *stethoscope*. It enables doctors to listen to air moving through a person's lungs, and to the opening and closing of heart valves. Knowing what healthy lungs and hearts sound like, doctors can listen for unusual sounds caused by infection or injury.

The *microphone*, invented in 1876, has many uses. It is a device, like the cochlea of your inner ear, that changes sound waves into electrical signals. Sometimes these signals are sent to a loudspeaker, where the process is reversed: Electrical messages cause a cone in the speaker to vibrate, sending out sound waves.

Microphones can be used to help record the complex songs of whales and other sounds people normally do not hear. Researchers once used special microphones to capture the ultrasounds of bats. Now anyone can buy a device to listen on a summer night as bats emit ultrasounds while zooming after insects.

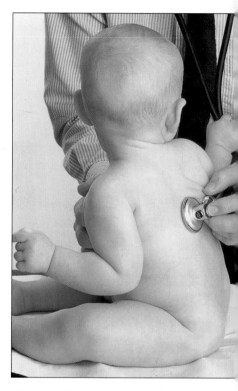

The stethoscope was the first device that enabled doctors to listen to a person's heart and lungs at work.

Extending Our Hearing

Ultrasounds are also used in undersea exploration. Ships use *sonar* systems to avoid obstacles, locate sunken wrecks, find schools of fish, and to measure water depth. In sonar, sound waves are sent into the water and their echoes are used to produce images of what lies below.

In medicine, sounds that we cannot hear are transmitted into a patient's body, and echoes of the sounds are changed into a picture on a screen. Doctors look at ultrasound pictures of a woman's womb to check on the health of the fetus or to see if twins are developing. Your first baby picture may have been an ultrasound image.

As the future family of a developing baby watches, reflected sound waves produce a picture on a screen of the fetus in its mother's womb.

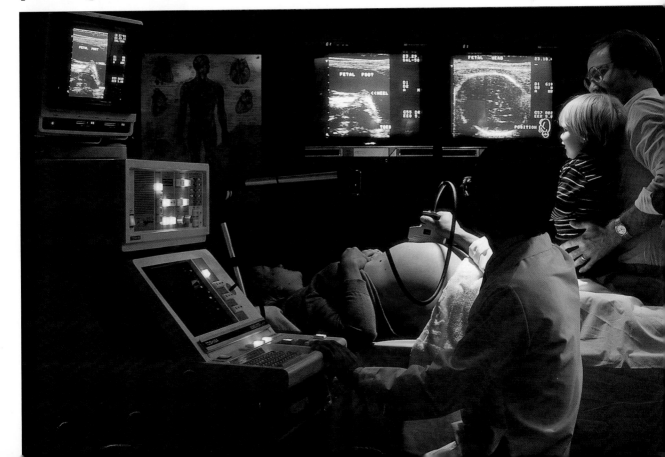

Helen Keller was famous for her struggle to live a full life while being both blind and deaf. She said, "I am just as deaf as I am blind. The problems of deafness are deeper and more complex." She called her lack of hearing "a much worse misfortune" because it robbed her of the sound of voices, and the give and take of conversation.

Everyone suffers some loss of their sense of hearing as they grow older. This is normal. You can avoid more serious loss of hearing by avoiding situations where you are exposed to lots of loud noise. This includes being careful while using stereo headphones. Loud sounds from these devices blast directly into your ear canals. Playing music loudly can destroy some of the hair cells of the organ of Corti.

Working in very noisy surroundings can also destroy hair cells. People exposed to four hours or more a day of 95 decibels are likely to suffer permanent harm to their hearing. Earplugs or padded ear protectors are vital to guard the precious sense of hearing.

From headphones or farther away, loud sounds can harm a person's sense of hearing.

Some hearing loss is temporary, and easily restored. Earwax or a small object may block the ear canal and keep sound waves from reaching the eardrum. Or the ear canal or middle ear may become infected. Doctors have simple and painless ways of solving these problems.

Damage to the inner ear is much more serious,

Taking Care of Your Hearing

because this is where sound vibrations are changed to nerve impulses and sent to the brain. Both hearing and balance can be affected. Once hair cells die they are not replaced. A hearing aid may help. These devices contain a tiny microphone, amplifier, and loudspeaker. Modern hearing aids fit right inside the ear canal.

Some damaged parts of the ear can be repaired by surgery. Sometimes extra bone grows around the stirrup bone of the middle ear, preventing it from passing along vibrations to the inner ear. A delicate operation can free the stirrup bone. An artificial stirrup bone can also be put in.

Remember, your ears give you both a sense of balance and the rich sounds of the world. Whether or not you agree with Helen Keller that hearing is the most vital sense, it clearly needs to be well guarded.

Anne Sullivan, right, was the teacher of Helen Keller, who was both blind and deaf. Helen Keller felt that being unable to hear was worse than being blind.

amplify—to make larger or stronger, as in amplifying a sound.

amplitude—the distance from the top to the bottom of a wave, including sound waves.

anvil—one of three tiny bones in the middle ear that help amplify vibrations of the eardrum.

auditory nerve—the nerve that carries messages about sounds from the inner ear to the brain.

auricles—the outer fleshy parts of our hearing system, commonly called the ears, through which sound waves enter the head. Ears are also called pinnae.

cartilage—strong but flexible tissue that makes up most of the outer ear, or auricle. Most of your nose is also made of cartilage.

cerumen—earwax, given off by tiny glands in the ear canal. Cerumen helps protect delicate ear parts by trapping bits of dust and dirt that enter the ear canal.

cochlea—the fluid-filled coiled structure in the inner ear in which vibrations from sound waves are changed to nerve messages that are sent to the brain.

decibel—the common unit used to measure the loudness or intensity of a sound. A decibel is one-tenth of a bel, a larger unit named for inventor Alexander Graham Bell.

eardrum—a thin membrane that is stretched tightly across the inside end of the outer ear canal. Sound waves cause the eardrum to vibrate, and the vibrations are passed on to parts of the inner ear.

eustachian tube—a narrow tube that connects the middle ear to the throat. It helps protect hearing by allowing air pressure within the ear to equal air pressure outside.

fetus—in humans, the unborn young from age two months to birth.

frequency—the number of waves, including sound waves, reaching a point in one second. Frequency is measured in hertz.

gravity—a natural force that causes objects to move toward the center of the Earth. Gravity causes objects to fall, and gives them weight.

hammer—one of three tiny bones in the middle ear that amplify the vibrations of the eardrum.

hertz—the unit of sound wave frequency. Children hear in the range of 20 to 20,000 hertz.

Glossary

infrasounds—sounds below the hearing range of humans.

larynx—the upper part of a person's windpipe, where the vocal cords are located.

lymph—the clear fluid that fills the cochlea and semicircular canals of the inner ear.

microphone—a device that changes sound waves into electric impulses.

organ of Corti—a strip of sensory cells in the cochlea that receives vibrations and changes them to nerve messages that are sent to the brain.

otoliths—tiny but heavy crystals in part of the inner ear that respond to the pull of gravity, and help you tell up from down.

oval window—a thin membrane between the middle and inner ears. Vibrations from the stirrup bone are passed on to the oval window.

pinnae—see auricles.

saccule—a part of the inner ear in which gravity and the position of a person's head are sensed.

semicircular canals—three curved tubes of the inner ear that contain fluid and hair cells, and that help you keep your balance.

skirl—the distinctive shrill tone produced by a bagpipe.

sonar—a system that emits sound waves, then receives reflections, or echoes, of the waves to form pictures. Sonar is used by ships and submarines to locate objects underwater.

stethoscope—a device that amplifies sound waves; used for listening to the working of the heart and other sounds produced within the body.

stirrup—one of three tiny bones in the middle ear that help amplify the vibrations of the eardrum.

temporal lobes—parts of the brain, located just behind the ears, where most sound memories are stored.

ultrasounds—sounds above the hearing range of humans.

utricle—a part of the inner ear in which gravity and the position of a person's head are sensed.

wavelength—the distance between two matching points of a wave, for example, from one peak to the next peak of a sound wave.

Index

Page numbers for illustrations are in boldface.

age factor, 11, 28
airplanes, 7, 13, 17
air pressure, 17
amplification, 16, 18, 30
amplitude, 10, 30
anvil bone, 16, **16**, **18**, 30
auditory nerve, **18**, 19, 30
auricles, 14, 30

bagpipes, 4, 31
balance, **22**, 22-23
bats, 4, 25, 26
bel, 12
birds, 24
bones, 16, **16**, **18**, 30
Boyle, Robert, 6, **6**
brain, 8, 19-21, 22

cartilage, 14, 30
cerumen, 15, 28, 30
children, 9, 11
clapping, 6
cochlea, 18, **18**
Corti, Alfonso, 19
crickets, **5**
crocodiles, 25

danger, 4
deafness, 12, 28-29
decibel, 12-13, **13**, 30
dizziness, 23
dogs, 11

ear
    inner, **18**, 19, **22**, 22-23, 28-29
    middle, 16-17, 28
    outer, 14-15
    protecting, 28
ear canal, 14-15, 28
eardrum, 15, 16, 17, **18**, 24, 30

earplugs, 28
ears
    hearing with both, 21
    movable, 14, **14**
elephants, 4, 25
Eustachian tubes, 17, 30

females, 9, 24
fetus, 20, **21**, 27, **27**, 30
fish, 6
flute, 10, **11**
forest riddle, 14
frequency, 10, 26

gravity, 23, 30

hair cells, 19, **19**, 23, 28
hammer bone, 16, **16**, **18**, 30
headphones, **28**
hearing, 14-21
    with both ears, 21
    development in humans, **21**
    human range of, 10-11, 25, 26
    loss or damage, 12, 28, **28**
hearing aids, 29
heart, 26
hertz, 10, 30
Hertz, Heinrich, 10
high-pitched sounds, 8, 9, 10
horizon, 23

infections, 28
infrasound, 25, 31

Keller, Helen, 28, **29**

larynx, 8, 31

light, 7
lightning, **7**
loudness, 10, 12-13, 16, 28, **28**
lungs, 26
lymph, 18, 23, 31

males, **5**, 9, 24
medicine, 27, 28. *See also* surgery
medulla, 20
memory, 20-21
microphones, 26, 31
motion, 23
mouth, 9
muscles, 8, 9, 16
music, 10, 12, 28

nature, 4
nerve impulses, 8, 20
noise pollution, 12

organ of Corti, **18**, 19, **19**, 28, 31
otoliths, 22-23, 31
oval window, 16, 18, 31
owls, 10, **24**, 24-25

pain, 13, 17
pinnae, 14, 30

rabbits, **14**
riddle, 14, 24
rock music, 12

saccule, 22, 31
safety, 4, 20
semicircular canals, 22, 31
sight, 23
skirl, 4, 31
sonar systems, 27, 31
sounds, 4, **5**

direction of, 14, **14**, 21
    from each ear, 21
    high and low frequency, 10
    high-pitched, 8
    number recognized, 20-21
sound waves, 6
    becoming sound, 24
    in hearing, 14, 18-20
    measurement, 10
    in microphones, 26
    in speaking, 8-9
    speed of, 7, **7**
speaking, 8-9
stethoscopes, 26, **26**, 31
stirrup bone, 16, **16**, 18, **18**, 29, 31
Sullivan, Anne, **29**
surgery, 29

teenage boys, 9
temporal lobes, 20, 31
tongue, 9
tuba, 10, **11**

ultrasound, 25, 26, 27, **27**, 31
undersea exploration, 27
utricle, 22, 31

vocal cords, 8, 9

walking, 22-23
water, 6-7, 26, 27
wavelength, 10, 31
wax, 15, 28, 30
whales, 26
whispers, 12, 16
whistles, 10, 11
workplace, 12, 28